The Best 50
SUMMER SOUPS

Hannah Suhr

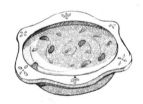

Bristol Publishing Enterprises
Hayward, California

Printed in the United States of America.
ISBN: 978-1-55867-332-8

Cover design: Frank J. Paredes
Cover photography: John A. Benson
Food Styling: Randy Mon
Illustration: Caryn Leschen

SOUPER-FOOD

Summer soups are quite different from traditional soups. Light, healthy, and often requiring little or no cooking, they are becoming an extremely popular choice as their versatility and health benefits become more widely known. Perfect for light lunches, first courses and even desserts, summer soups have developed into a completely separate category from their winter counterparts. If you've got a food processor or blender, the world of summer soups is waiting to be discovered.

Many diets use soup as the primary focus. There are a few fundamental reasons for this. The additional liquid in soups both helps us feel more full and gets us to eat more slowly, which is excellent for proper digestion; the optimal balance of fat, protein and carbs happens naturally without excessive measuring or feelings of deprivation; and ingredients tend naturally to be healthy, lowfat, and full of nutrients. We can also add additional produce, meat, fish and/or carbs to the broth.

Summer soups take the health benefits of soup one step further. As these soups are often prepared with little or no cooking, they retain the most vitamins and minerals possible from their ingredients. Nonfat yogurt often replaces heavy cream. Fresh fish can be lightly steamed in the soup pot, not sautéed in heavy butter or oil. Most of the summer soups in this book can be finished off with a drizzle of good extra virgin olive oil if desired. Olive oil is a healthy unsaturated fat and actually aids in the absorption of nutrients from many fresh greens.

All clear broths and teas in this book can be served unclouded as a base for garnishes. Clear broths are generally prepared and seasoned separately from other ingredients and assembled right before serving. They should never be left to sit for long periods of time with starchy ingredients such as pasta or potatoes as they will cloud up and lose their appeal.

TIPS FOR SERVING SUMMER SOUPS

- Summer soups should be served chilled or warmed, never steaming hot. Recipes include a recommendation for serving temperature.
- Raw soups and broths, where ingredients have not blended with heat, should often rest to allow flavors to blend properly.
- If soups intended to be served chilled are refrigerated for more than an hour, they should be removed from the fridge 30 minutes before serving. Chilled means cool, not icy cold.
- Many fruit soups are intended to be served very cold or icy. Such recipes will note this intent.
- Soups thicken as they cool, so careful attention must be paid to adding enough liquid.
- Add any olive oil right before serving chilled soups, so the oil

won't solidify in the refrigerator.

- Always check seasonings again before serving, as the relationships between certain flavors will change during cooling.

- Any soup base that is mostly chicken stock will be best served warm. A little bit in a puree can still be served chilled, but be careful of chicken fat coagulation. Homemade broths should be chilled and skimmed before using in these recipes.

- The difference between broth and stock is a common gray area. Stock is made from meat and bones and has a gelatinous quality when chilled. For this reason, broth (which is made without bones) should always be used in summer soups.

- Leafy herbs like basil, cilantro and parsley should be added toward the end. If sauteed for too long they lose flavor.

PLATING/PRESENTATION

Keep a few tips in mind to make your soups attractive.

Garnishes like herbed noodles and fruit salsas should emerge from the center of the soup, providing texture and contrasting color. If broth is thin, pile garnish in the center of the bowl and pour soup around it, leaving part above the surface of the liquid. Purees are thick, so garnishes may be added safely at the end.

Also, summer soups are intended to be a feast for the eye as well as the palate, so try to have the color of your dish complement your soup. Shallow, wide bowls allow for deep garnishes to emerge properly, and white rims are a safe bet.

HERB GARNISHES

Tearing basil leaves releases aroma without bruising the leaves and offers an appealing, rustic look. Leaves should always be torn from stems: herb stems can be used in some cases, but are too bitter and coarsely textured for delicate soups. Rosemary stems make great skewers for grilling seafood or chicken.

CRISPED PROSCIUTTO

Prosciutto is a high-quality Italian cured ham, often served in salads or with melon. It's a sophisticated substitute for bacon.

prosciutto (Italian cured ham)

Slice prosciutto into thin strips. Sauté over medium heat until crisp. Drain on paper towels.

PARMESAN WAFERS

These thin, salty crisps are made entirely from cheese.

grated fresh parmesan cheese   paprika
black pepper

For each wafer, heap 3 tbs. cheese on a nonstick cookie sheet. Dust with with pepper and paprika. Bake at 375° for 10 minutes. Form into shapes over cups or bowls, or leave flat to harden.

GARLIC CROUTONS

A savory soup staple. These crisp garlicky cubes finish off just about any savory soup perfectly.

¼ cup extra virgin olive oil or butter
1 clove garlic, minced
3 thick slices French bread, cut into cubes
salt

Heat oven to 350°. In a pan, melt oil or butter over medium heat. Stir in garlic; cook and stir for 1 minute. Add bread cubes, and toss to coat. Spread on a baking sheet.

Bake for about 15 minutes, until crisp and dry. Check frequently to prevent burning. Cool.

INFUSED OILS

Infused oils add great flavor and color to summer soups. They are most optimally used with cool or room temperature foods so as not to disturb the character of the herbs. Infused oils can be made in many different ways, but this method ensures the strongest flavor and brightest color. It will not store as long as other varieties though, and should be made in small quantities.

herb leaves
grapeseed or canola oil

Bruise herb leaves (such as mint or basil). Cover with grapeseed or canola oil. Warm in skillet until leaves are soft. Puree until leaves turn oil green. Let rest for 1 day to 2 weeks. Strain through cheesecloth and serve. Refrigerate remaining oil in a sealed container for 2 to 3 weeks.

BASIC QUESADILLA COOKING INSTRUCTIONS

Adapt these directions according to the recipe suggestions accompanying many of the gazpacho recipes. Temperatures will not be high enough to cook raw foods, so make sure meats are cooked before assembling. Wet ingredients (tomatoes, fruits, sauces) will affect the texture of the finished product, so use sparingly.

8–12 corn or flour tortillas
1/2 lb. Monterey Jack cheese
other ingredients as specified

Heat griddle or pan over medium heat. Use oil if desired; it adds crispness and flavor, but omit if watching your diet. Spread ingredients evenly on tortilla. Sandwich second tortilla on top. Grill in pan until tortilla is crisp and brown. Flip and continue cooking until second side is brown and cheese is melted. Slice into 6 segments with a pizza cutter or large knife.

BASIC GAZPACHO

Cool, fresh and spicy. Gazpacho is a traditional summer favorite.

½ lb. ripe tomatoes, peeled, seeded and chopped
2 cloves garlic, finely chopped
1 tbs. finely chopped jalapeño pepper, seeds removed
½ cucumber, peeled, seeded and diced
½ red bell pepper, seeded and diced
½ small red onion, diced
2 cups chicken stock

2 cups tomato juice
juice of 1 lime
2 tbs. red wine vinegar
¼ cup basil, cut into long strips
¼ cup flat leaf parsley, finely chopped
¼ cup cilantro, finely chopped
salt and pepper
extra virgin olive oil

Combine all ingredients in a large glass bowl. Do not use a metal bowl, as the metal reacts with the acid in the tomatoes. Add salt and pepper to taste. Add more tomato juice if necessary to cover vegetables. Chill in the refrigerator. Drizzle with extra virgin olive oil before serving. Serve cool with *Chicken Quesadilla,* follows.

CHICKEN QUESADILLA
1 can refried pinto beans
$1/4$ cup chopped fresh cilantro, or to taste
shredded chicken

Combine ingredients and follow *Basic Quesadilla Cooking Instructions,* page 9.

ROASTED TOMATO GAZPACHO

Serves 4–6

The tomato is the most common base for hot or cold soups. Tomato seeds can be bitter so gently squeeze tomatoes before roasting or pureeing. Plum tomatoes have the fewest seeds, but also the least liquid, so adjust ingredients accordingly. Grape and cherry tomatoes are sweetest. Yellow tomatoes are low acid. Heirloom are harder to find and more expensive but have fantastic flavors especially when used raw in salsas and gazpachos.

1 lb. tomatoes, any variety
5–6 cloves garlic, whole
1 small yellow onion, diced
salt
extra virgin olive oil
1 small red pepper, whole
1/2 cup fresh basil, chopped
1/2 cup fresh parsley, chopped
juice of 1 lemon
2 cups chicken stock
2 cups tomato juice
1/2 tsp. red pepper flakes
salt and pepper to taste

Preheat broiler. In a 9 x 9 baking dish add tomatoes (note: cherry tomatoes can be left whole; plum tomatoes should be halved or quartered; beefsteak should be quartered and squeezed to eliminate some seeds). Add garlic and onion. Salt liberally. Drizzle with extra virgin olive oil and toss gently. Broil until soft and starting to blacken, stirring occasionally. Remove and cool.

Roast red pepper on oven burner, allowing skin to blacken completely and insides to soften. Once cool, skin will slide off easily.

In the food processor combine tomato mixture, basil, parsley, roasted pepper, lemon juice, chicken stock, tomato juice and red pepper flakes. Pulse until smooth, add more stock and juice if necessary to achieve a smooth, thin puree.

Taste and add salt and pepper as desired. Serve warm or cool.

TUSCAN SUMMER TOMATO SOUP

Serves 4–6

A classic combination of white beans and rosemary is lightened up with a basic roasted tomato broth. The result: a timeless and healthy Italian summer soup. Serve at room temperature with a drizzle of extra virgin olive oil, fresh rosemary and Parmesan wafers.

Roasted Tomato Gazpacho, page 11
2 tbs. fresh rosemary, chopped
1 cup cooked white beans

Make the *Roasted Tomato Gazpacho* recipe as on page 11, but omit parsley and basil. Instead, add 2 tbs. fresh rosemary to the food processor. Add 1 cup cooked white beans at end—do not process. Serve warm.

ROASTED TOMATO GAZPACHO WITH CRAB AND CORN SALSA

Serves 4–6

California cuisine blends the American farmstand with ethnic influences. Light, healthy and flavorful, this Californian soup is true fusion. Serve cold with a drizzle of extra virgin olive oil a squeeze of lime and a cheese quesadilla.

Roasted Tomato Gazpacho, page 11

CRAB AND CORN SALSA

$1/2$ cup lump crab meat
fresh kernels of 3 corn cobs
$1/2$ small red onion, diced
cracked pepper

$1/2$ tsp. salt
juice of $1/2$ lime
1 tsp. red wine vinegar
fresh cilantro

Gently combine all ingredients. Garnish roasted tomato soup with a few tablespoons of crab and corn salsa. Serve cool.

GREEK FETA AND KALAMATA GAZPACHO

Serves 4–6

As many of the ingredients in the basic gazpacho are also traditionally Greek, this adaptation is very simple to accomplish. Serve this with Greek Quesadilla, page 17.

½ lb. ripe tomatoes, peeled
½ cucumber
½ red bell pepper
1 medium jalapeño pepper
2 cloves garlic, finely chopped
½ small red onion, diced
2 cups chicken stock
2 cups tomato juice
juice of 1 lime
2 tbs. red wine vinegar

¼ cup basil, cut into strips
½ cup chopped spinach leaves
¼ cup flat leaf parsley, finely chopped
¼ cup fresh mint, finely chopped
½ cup sliced, pitted kalamata olives
salt and pepper
extra virgin olive oil

Remove seeds and chop tomatoes, cucumber, bell pepper and jalapeños. Be careful not to wipe your eyes after handling jalapeño seeds. Combine with onion, stock, tomato juice, lime juice, vinegar, basil, parsley, spinach, mint and olives in a large glass bowl. Do not use a metal bowl, as the metal reacts with the acid in the tomatoes.

Add salt and pepper to taste. Add more tomato juice if necessary to cover vegetables. Chill in the refrigerator. Drizzle with extra virgin olive oil before serving. Garnish with crumbled feta, a mint sprig and cracked pepper. Serve cool.

GREEK QUESADILLA

feta cheese   garlic, finely diced
chopped fresh spinach leaves

Follow *Basic Quesadilla Cooking Instructions*, page 9.

CALIFORNIA GAZPACHO WITH SEARED SHRIMP AND AVOCADO

Serves 4–6

Shrimp and avocado make cool and hearty accompaniments to a light and spicy gazpacho. Serve with Tuscany Quesadilla, *page 19.*

½ lb. ripe tomatoes, peeled
½ cucumber
½ red bell pepper
1 medium jalapeño pepper
2 cloves garlic, finely chopped
½ small red onion, diced
2 cups chicken stock
2 cups tomato juice
juice of 1 lime

2 tbs. red wine vinegar
¼ cup basil, cut into strips
¼ cup flat leaf parsley, finely chopped
¼ cup fresh mint, finely chopped
salt and pepper
extra virgin olive oil

SEARED SHRIMP

1–1½ lb. jumbo shrimp,
   peeled and deveined
juice of 1 lime

1 tsp. salt
extra virgin olive oil
1 ripe, firm avocado, diced

Marinate shrimp in lime juice and salt for 15 minutes. Toss in extra virgin olive oil. Sear over medium-high heat for 3 minutes on each side. Combine avocado with shrimp. Pile in center of gazpacho, top with cracked pepper. Serve warm or cool.

TUSCANY QUESADILLA

smashed white beans
2 oz. chèvre goat cheese

chopped fresh parsley to taste
2 sprigs fresh rosemary

Follow *Basic Quesadilla Cooking Instructions,* page 9.

YELLOW GAZPACHO WITH AVOCADO

Serves 4–6

Using chicken stock keeps the yellow color. Serve lightly warmed: do not overheat, or the soup will lose its texture. Serve with Tex-Mex Quesadillas, *page 21.*

4 cups chicken stock
2 cloves garlic, finely diced
1 lb. yellow tomatoes, peeled, seeded and chopped
1/2 cucumber, peeled, seeded and chopped
1/2 red onion, finely diced
juice of 1 lime
1–2 ripe, firm avocados, diced
1 tbs. extra virgin olive oil
salt and pepper to taste

Simmer chicken broth over low heat with garlic. Combine remaining ingredients in a large glass bowl. Pour garlicky broth over tomato mixture and serve warm.

TEX-MEX QUESADILLA
1 can smashed or refried pinto beans
2 cups cooked, pulled bbq pork

Combine ingredients and follow *Basic Quesadilla Cooking Instructions*, page 9.

GREEN GAZPACHO

In an unusual touch, the heat allows for white wine to be added here. Serve this warm with Spicy Shrimp Quesadillas, *page 23.*

½ lb. green tomatoes
½ cucumber, peeled
1 medium jalapeño
2 tbs. extra virgin olive oil
½ small yellow onion, diced
2 cloves garlic, finely chopped
4 cups chicken stock

¼ cup white wine
½ lb. tomatillos, diced
¼ cup green onion, chopped
¼ cup cilantro, finely chopped
squeeze of lime to taste
salt and pepper

Seed and dice tomatoes, cucumbers, and jalapeños. Heat oil in a medium skillet. Add onion and garlic and sauté until soft. Add chicken stock and wine and simmer for 5 minutes.

Add remaining ingredients and warm through for 1 minute. Serve immediately.

SPICY SHRIMP QUESADILLA
Seared Shrimp, page 19
2 oz. chèvre goat cheese
1 fresh jalapeño, finely chopped
¼ cup finely chopped fresh cilantro

Combine ingredients and follow *Basic Quesadilla Cooking Instructions,* page 9.

TROPICAL GAZPACHO

Chill this fresh tropical fruit salsa overnight and add juice to make a wonderful healthy soup. Serve cold for breakfast with yogurt and honey or for dessert with traditional anise pizelles (available in the bakery section of some grocery stores) and whipped cream.

1 fresh pineapple, diced	juice of 1 lime
1 mango, diced	3 cups cranberry juice
½ papaya, diced	1 cup fresh pomegranate seeds
1 tbs. honey	mint sprigs for garnish

Combine pineapple, mango and papaya. Toss with honey and lime. Set aside for 1 hour or overnight.

Add cranberry juice to mixture. Garnish and serve with pomegranate seeds and mint. Serve cold.

VICHYSSOISE AND OTHER POTATO SOUPS

Traditional vichyssoise is a chilled French potato leek soup with cream. By replacing the cream with lowfat yogurt and adding new fresh ingredients, this traditional summer soup is made healthy and updated.

Unlike many of our other summer soups, potato soups still require a two step process, simmering, then chilling. If prepared the day before, this light meal is ready to serve very quickly.

Most of the garnishes in these recipes are interchangeable, so try crumbled chèvre with the *Herbed Sweet Potato Vichyssoise,* page 29, or skewered shrimp with the *Chilled Pesto-Potato Gazpacho,* page 32, or try your own variation with the freshest ingredients you can find. Serve any of these soups either warm or cooled.

LIGHT VICHYSSOISE WITH LEMON

Serves 4–6

Try to use Yukon Gold potatoes if possible, for their flavor and yellow colored flesh.

2 tbs. extra virgin olive oil
4 large leeks, chopped, white parts only
1 medium potato, diced
3–4 cloves garlic, crushed
4 cups chicken broth
$\frac{1}{2}$ cup lowfat plain yogurt
salt and pepper
chives for garnish
juice and grated zest of 1 lemon

Heat oil over medium heat. Add leeks. Cook until soft but not brown.

Lower heat if browning begins. Add potato and garlic. Stir in broth. Simmer for 30 minutes, or until potatoes are soft. Cool.

Puree in a food processor until smooth. Add yogurt and puree again. Season with salt and pepper. Chill overnight.

Serve with crusty bread. Garnish with snipped chives and lemon juice and zest. Serve cool.

VICHYSSOISE WITH SHRIMP AND CHÈVRE Serves 4–6

The sweet shrimp and tart chèvre add excellent flavor and texture to this classic soup.

Light Vichyssoise with Lemon, page 26
1 tbs. chopped fresh rosemary
1 lb. jumbo shrimp, peeled and deveined
olive oil for tossing
1 pinch nutmeg
$\frac{1}{2}$ cup crumbled chèvre goat cheese

Make *Light Vichyssoise with Lemon* as on page 26, but add rosemary to the soup before pureeing.

Toss shrimp with olive oil and nutmeg. Skewer on rosemary stems and grill until curled and pink, about 3 minutes each side. Cool shrimp. Place whole skewer into soup and serve cool with crumbled chèvre.

HERBED SWEET POTATO VICHYSSOISE

Serves 4–6

Here is a sweet and summery twist to a classic soup.

Light Vichyssoise with Lemon, page 26
1 medium sweet potato
2 tbs. chopped fresh chives
2 tbs. chopped fresh flat-leaf parsley
chives for garnish

Make *Light Vichyssoise with Lemon* as on page 26, but replace potato with sweet potato. Add chives and parsley before pureeing. Garnish with snipped chives. Serve cool.

SPICED SWEET POTATO PUREE

Serves 4–6

This warm and comforting soup works with a light salad in the summer and as a side for pork roast in the fall and winter. Garnish with cracked pepper and a goat cheese medallion and/or torn basil

2 medium sweet potatoes, whole
1 small shallot, chopped
½ tsp. cinnamon
½ tsp. salt
juice of ½ lemon
2 tsp. honey

4 cups chicken stock
½ cup orange juice
extra virgin olive oil
salt and fresh cracked pepper
crumbled chèvre goat cheese for garnish
basil for garnish

Bake sweet potatoes until soft and sugar begins to caramelize, about 45 minutes.

Cool sweet potatoes and remove skin. Puree shallot in food processor. Add sweet potatoes, cinnamon, salt, lemon juice, honey, chicken stock, orange juice, and a drizzle of extra virgin olive oil. Puree until smooth; add more stock if necessary.

Season to taste with salt and pepper. Garnish with chèvre and basil. Serve warm.

CHILLED PESTO-POTATO GAZPACHO

Serves 4–6

The flavors of pesto thrive in warm temperatures. Serve this with Crisped Prosciutto, *page 6, and a green salad.*

½ tsp. salt	¼ cup *Pesto Sauce,* page 33
4 cups chicken stock	chopped basil for garnish
2 Yukon Gold potatoes, cubed	cracked pepper
1 small yellow onion, cubed	shaved parmesan for garnish

Add salt to chicken stock. Simmer potatoes and onion in salted broth for about 30 minutes, until potatoes are soft. Spoon out half of the cubed potatoes and set aside. Puree remaining ingredients with half of the pesto.

Toss remaining potatoes in remaining pesto. Pile in center of each bowl. Pour potato puree around cubed potatoes. Garnish with basil, pepper and shaved parmesan. Serve warm.

PESTO SAUCE
2 cups fresh basil, packed
$1/2$ cup olive oil
3 cloves garlic
3 tbs. pine nuts
$1/2$ cup grated parmesan cheese
3 tbs. grated romano cheese
salt and pepper to taste

Rinse and pat dry basil leaves. Remove leaves from stems. Add olive oil, basil leaves, garlic, pine nuts, salt and pepper to food processor. Pulse and scrape down sides of processor with a spatula until smooth. Stir in grated cheeses. Add a little more olive oil if needed for mixture to blend properly. Test seasoning and adjust to taste.

HERB AND VEGETABLE PUREES

The textures of purees lend themselves well to chilling. The quality of ingredients determines the quality of your puree. Try to find seasonal produce at farmers markets as often as possible. Organic is also a great way to go, not only for the quality of ingredients but for the contribution they make to the environment.

Purees should have a single top ingredient with secondary supporting seasonings, similar to a perfume. Too many ingredients will muddle your flavors and/or colors.

Never contrast colors in your ingredients, as a murky-colored puree, no matter how flavorful, will not be appealing. When pureeing ingredients in the food processor, occasionally stop and scrape down the sides of the processor with a spatula to make sure mixture blends well.

CUCUMBER PUREE
WITH YOGURT AND MINT

Serves 4–6

This light Greek fusion soup can be served as a starter, as a palate cleanser for an elaborate meal, or with spanakopita for a light lunch or dinner.

1 large cucumber, peeled,
    seeded and diced
1/2 cup lowfat plain yogurt
1/4 cup fresh mint
1/4 cup dill, chopped
juice of 1 lemon

3 cups chicken stock
1 tbs. white wine vinegar
1 tbs. honey
salt and pepper
mint sprig for garnish

Puree all ingredients until smooth. Pulse and scrape down sides of processor occasionally. Garnish with a fresh mint sprig. Serve cold.

GUACAMOLE SOUP

Serves 4–6

Rich and smooth, there is nothing like the texture of avocado. The color will begin to change quickly, even with the necessary citrus juice added, so serve immediately after preparing. Garnish with tortilla chips, chopped tomatoes and a splash of lime.

3 ripe avocados, peeled and
  pitted
2 cloves garlic, chopped
1/4 cup chopped cilantro
juice of 1 lime

2 tomatillos, cleaned and
  chopped
2 green tomatoes, chopped
3 cups chicken stock
salt and pepper

Puree all ingredients in a blender. Pulse and scrape down sides of processor occasionally. Serve immediately. Serve cool or at room temperature.

FRESH GREEN PEA SOUP

Serves 4–6

A lighter and brighter variation of a traditional pea soup, this one is perfect for summer. Plain yogurt adds a smoother texture and mint is an unexpected complement to the peas. Do not overdo the mint.

1 small yellow onion, chopped	1 lb. frozen peas
extra virgin olive oil	½ cup plain nonfat yogurt
2 cloves garlic, crushed	2–3 tbs. fresh mint, chopped
2 cups chicken stock	salt and pepper

Slice onion thinly and sauté in oil over medium heat until soft. Add crushed garlic and sauté for 1 more minute. Pour in chicken stock and bring to a boil. Add peas and boil for 3 minutes. Pour mixture into food processor with mint leaves, salt and pepper to taste, and yogurt. Puree until smooth. Pulse and scrape down sides of processor occasionally. Chill. Serve with garlic croutons and torn basil. Serve warm or cool.

CHILLED CARROT PUREE

Serves 4–6

Using carrot juice in addition to chicken stock makes this one perfect for serving cold. Serve with sprouted wheat bread for a light and healthy lunch.

1 small yellow onion, diced
extra virgin olive oil
2 cloves garlic, crushed
2 cups chicken stock
3 large carrots, chopped

1/4 cup fresh dill, chopped
2 cups carrot juice
1/2 tsp. grated fresh ginger
salt and pepper

Slice onion thinly and sauté in oil over medium heat until soft. Add crushed garlic and sauté for 1 more minute. Pour in chicken stock and bring to a boil. Add carrots and boil until soft. Pour mixture into a food processor with dill and carrot juice. Add ginger and salt and pepper to taste. Puree until smooth. Pulse and scrape down sides of processor occasionally. Chill. Serve cold.

CORN PUREE WITH CRAB AND CORN SALSA   Serves 4–6

Corn on the cob is the quintessential summer vegetable. Frozen corn may be substituted for fresh in the puree if fresh corn isn't available, but it is not recommended for the salsa.

1 tbs. sugar	2 cups chicken stock
1½ tbs. salt, divided	1 cup fresh basil, cut into strips
8–9 fresh ears of corn,	cracked pepper
shucked and cleaned	*Crab and Corn Salsa*, page 15

Bring a full pot of water to a boil. Stir in sugar and 1 tbs. of the salt. Add shucked corn. Turn water off and let sit for 5 minutes. Remove corn and plunge into cold water. Slice kernels from cobs. Reserve half of the corn for salsa. Combine remainder of corn with chicken stock, basil, remaining salt and cracked pepper. Puree until smooth.

Serve this with *Crab and Corn Salsa*, page 15.

MUSHROOM AND HERB PUREE

Serves 4–6

The flavor combination of browned mushrooms, sherry and garlic is timeless, rich and versatile. Serve with thin slices of cooled steak or parmesan herbed vermicelli (see below) and a green salad for a little bit of winter comfort on a hot summers day.

1lb assorted mushrooms
    (cremini, shitake, morel,
    oyster, portobello)
2 tbs. extra virgin olive oil
2 cloves garlic, chopped

¼ cup sherry
3 cups chicken stock
½ cup finely chopped fresh
    parsley
salt and pepper to taste

Sauté mushrooms in extra virgin olive oil until all water has evaporated and browning begins. Add sherry and chopped garlic. Continue cooking for 3 to 4 minutes longer.

Add chicken stock, bring to boil and turn off heat. Cool for 5 minutes.

Combine mushroom mixture in a food processor with parsley and salt and pepper. Puree until smooth. Serve warm.

PARMESAN HERBED VERMICELLI
$1/2$ lb. vermicelli
2 tbs. extra virgin olive oil
$1/4$ cup finely chopped parsley and basil
$1/4$ cup fresh grated Parmigiano Reggiano

Boil pasta in heavily salted water until al dente (pasta is firm). Drain and toss with extra virgin olive oil, herbs and cheese. Twist into towers in shallow bowls. Pour mushroom mixture around pasta and serve immediately.

ZUCCHINI LEMON PUREE WITH SNAP PEAS   Serves 4–6

Snap peas add excellent color and texture contrast without detracting from the delicate flavor of the zucchini puree.

2 tbs. extra virgin olive oil
1/2 yellow onion, diced
2 cloves garlic, diced
4 cups chicken stock
2 large zucchini, chopped

1 cup snap peas
juice of 1/2 lemon
1/2 cup chopped flat leaf parsley
salt and pepper to taste
cracked pepper for garnish

Heat olive oil in a medium saucepan. Add onion and garlic and sauté until soft. Add chicken stock and bring to a simmer. Add zucchini and cook until beginning to soften (fork slips through easily). Allow to cool. Steam snap peas for about 3 minutes. Plunge into cold water to preserve color and texture. Puree zucchini mixture with lemon juice, parsley, salt and pepper. Serve warm, immediately with snap peas and cracked pepper.

SPICY TOMATILLO PUREE

Serves 4–6

With simpler, more melded flavors than the green gazpacho, this soup really allows the bite of the tomatillo to take center stage. Serve cool with garlic croutons.

8–10 tomatillos, chopped
2–3 green tomatoes, chopped (if available)
2–3 cloves garlic, whole
1/4 cup cilantro
3 cups chicken stock
salt and pepper to taste
extra virgin olive oil

Puree all ingredients but extra virgin olive oil until smooth. Serve immediately with a drizzle of extra virgin olive oil. Serve cool.

FRESH PLUM PUREE WITH ARMAGNAC

Serves 4–6

Plums and Armagnac are a classic french combination. Many plum purees are made with reconstituted dried plums (prunes) this fresh version captures the bright nuances in flavor of fresh plums and softens them with honey. Whichever type of plum you choose, keep consistent in color, all red, all green or all black. Add honey to taste as the acidity content can vary greatly.

2 cups water
1 lb. fresh plums, pitted and
    sliced

honey to taste
1/4 cup Armagnac brandy
black pepper

Boil water. Add plums to boiling water. Simmer and stir until soft. Add honey to taste. Add Armagnac. Add a few twists of black pepper. Puree mixture until smooth. Cool and serve with plain yogurt or vanilla whipped cream and mint. Serve cool.

STRAWBERRY PUREE

An unusual trick recently gone mainstream, balsamic vinegar enhances the flavor of a good strawberry ten-fold. Be careful not to overdo it as there's a thin line between subtle and overpowering. Serve a small amount in a shallow bowl with cracked pepper and or mint garnish and a dollop of strained greek yogurt drizzled with honey.

1 qt. fresh strawberries
juice of $\frac{1}{2}$ lemon
2 tbs. honey
$\frac{1}{2}$–1 tbs. balsamic vinegar
1 tbs. Cointreau orange liqueur

Puree all ingredients in a food processor. Chill for at least an hour, or up to overnight. Serve cold.

SUMMER SOUPS   45

WATERMELON PUREE WITH MINT OIL

Mint infused oil makes the perfect flavor and color partner for the hot pink watermelon puree. (see Infused Oils, *page 8)*

2 lbs. watermelon, cubed and seeded
1/2 lemon, juiced
2 tbs. honey
1/2 tsp. salt
Mint Infused Oil, page 8

Place watermelon, lemon juice, honey and salt in a blender container. Puree until smooth. Drizzle with mint oil. Serve cold.

SUMMER MELON WITH CHAMPAGNE

Serves 4–6

Any summer melons may be substituted here (casaba, Crenshaw, canary). Use whatever is fresh and available except watermelon, whose texture isn't properly compatible. This combination can also be sipped from a champagne flute: double the champagne; half the puree; stir, garnish and serve. In a dish, the champagne is a welcome surprise and adds to the body and subtlety of the soup.

½ lb. cantaloupe, cubed and seeded
½ lb. honeydew melon, cubed and seeded
juice and zest of ½ lemon
2 tbs. honey
1 cup Champagne
mint sprigs for garnish

Puree cantaloupe, melon, lemon juice and honey until smooth. Gently stir in champagne and lemon zest. Serve immediately with mint garnish.

GINGER PEACH

Like a Georgian summers day: serve with yogurt and honey for breakfast, or with Cinnamon-Scented Whipped Cream *for dessert.*

2 lbs. fresh peaches
2 cups water
1 tsp. grated fresh ginger
1/8 tsp. ground cloves
1 tbs. lemon juice

2 tbs. honey
1/2 tsp. salt
1 pint heavy cream
1/2 tsp. cinnamon
2 tbs. sugar

Pit and slice peaches. Combine with water and ginger in a medium saucepan. Simmer until peaches are soft. Puree half of the peaches with cloves, lemon, honey and salt. Stir in remaining peaches. Serve immediately. Serve warm or cool.

CINNAMON-SCENTED WHIPPED CREAM

Whip heavy cream with cinnamon and sugar until peaks form.

APRICOT ANISE

Serves 4–6

Anise is a complex and sophisticated liquorice flavor. Paired with the delicate sweetness of apricots, this soup will make a lasting impression.

1 lb. fresh apricots, pitted and sliced
2 tbs. honey
2 cups water
1 crushed star anise (or $\frac{1}{2}$ tsp. crushed anise seed)
1 tbs. sambuca or ouzo anise liqueur

In a medium saucepan, combine apricots, honey, water and star anise. Simmer until fruit is soft. Remove star anise. Cool slightly and puree with liquor until smooth.

Serve a small amount with a dollop of *Cinnamon-Scented Whipped Cream,* page 48. Serve cool.

LEMON GLASS BROTH WITH BERRIES

Serves 4–6

Lemon and honey here are not accents, but the flavor focus. Serve with plump summer berries. Frozen berries are not recommended as they will immediately bleed, discoloring the broth.

juice and zest of 6 lemons
½ cup honey
3 cups water
½ cup white wine
2 lemon tea bags

1 pint fresh berries (any combination blackberries, boysenberries or raspberries)
fresh mint

For *Lemon Glass Broth,* simmer juice and zest of lemons, honey, water and wine until most of the alcohol has evaporated, about 3 to 5 minutes. Turn off heat and add tea bags. Steep for 3 minutes. Discard bags and let cool.

Pour into shallow bowls and pile berries in center. Serve cool, with ginger or graham cookies and a dollop of whipped cream.

ROSÉ SANGRIA SOUP

Serves 4–6

Sangria, traditionally made with red wine, is now sometimes pre-pared with white or rosé wines, to make "white sangrias". Here we change this drink into a soup. The wine is cut with juice.

¼ cup brandy	2 peaches, pitted and diced
2 cups rosé wine	2 apricots, pitted and diced
1 cup apple juice	4–5 figs, quartered
¼ cup rose flower water	1 green apple, cubed
¼ cup honey	¼ tsp. cinnamon

Combine wine, juice, rose water and honey in a bowl. Stir until honey is dissolved and chill. Combine sliced fruits in another bowl. Drizzle with brandy until coated and dust with cinnamon. Soak brandied fruit for at least 1 hour. Spoon fruit into bowl. Pour broth around fruit. Serve with cinnamon cookies or anise cookies. Serve cool.

CANTALOUPE PUREE WITH LIME AND CRISPED PROSCIUTTO STRIPS

Serves 4–6

This adaptation of the classic hors d'oeuvre on a toothpick takes the flavor combination to the next level with lime, basil and the ingenious flavor and texture of crisping the prosciutto. Destined to be a new classic.

1 large cantaloupe, seeded and cubed
juice of $\frac{1}{2}$ lime
2 tbs. honey
5–6 thin slices prosciutto
fresh basil leaves

Puree cantaloupe, lime and honey until smooth. Slice thin strips of prosciutto and sauté until crisp (see *Crisped Prosciutto,* page 6). Drain prosciutto on paper towels. Top puree with prosciutto and torn basil leaves. Serve cool.

HONEYDEW PUREE WITH BASIL SCENTED OIL

The green on green presentation is pure elegance, but the unexpected flavor combination is what makes this soup a true signature dish.

1 large honeydew melon, seeded and cubed
juice of ½ lime
2 tbs. honey
basil oil (see *Infused Oils,* page 8)

Puree honeydew with lime and honey. Spoon into bowls and drizzle with basil oil. Serve immediately. Serve cool.

MANGO WITH CHILE OIL

A traditional Mexican treat, mango with chili powder and lime is sold on the streets of many urban Latino neighborhoods in the United States. The honey-sweet soft mango is contrasted simply and perfectly with the fiery chile and sharp lime. Chile oil is used for color and texture contrast but chili powder may be substituted if necessary. Serve as a first course to an elegant Mexican meal.

4 large mangoes, pitted and cubed
juice of ½ lime
Chile Infused Oil (see *Infused Oils,* page 8)

In a food processor or blender, puree mango and lime until smooth. Drizzle with chile oil. Serve cool.

FENNEL PUREE WITH ORANGES AND CHÈVRE

A classic salad combination melds its flavors exceptionally well in this simple preparation. Blood oranges or pink grapefruit may also be used.

1 bulb fresh fennel root, thinly sliced
3 cups chicken stock
½ tsp. salt
1 lb. oranges or grapefruit
1 tbs. extra virgin olive oil
cracked pepper
1 small log chèvre

Simmer fennel in chicken stock until soft. Add salt and puree until smooth. Peel and segment oranges so no white remains. Combine olive oil with segmented oranges and generous grinds of cracked pepper.

Pour puree into bowl. Pile clusters of oranges in center. Finish with a wedge of chèvre and a final grind of pepper. Serve cool.

HERBED ORANGE BROTH

Serves 4–6

Adapted from a traditional Haitian recipe, this simple soup serves as an elegant first course, and is rumored to clear up a summer cold.

1 cup chicken broth
2 cups orange juice
1 tbs. grated fresh ginger
3 large cloves garlic, whole
$1/2$ tsp. whole cloves
$1/4$ cup finely chopped Italian parsley

Simmer all ingredients except parsley, covered, for 20 to 30 minutes. Strain, cool slightly and stir in parsley: stirring parsley into steaming hot liquid will cause parsley to wilt and lose color. Serve warm with a floating slice of orange and a final pinch of parsley.

LEMON BROTH WITH VERMICELLI AND CAVIAR

Serve this classic appetizer as a first course. Simply coat the bottom of the bowl with the broth. The caviar should stick to the broth coated pasta, not get lost in the liquid itself.

2–3 tbs. salt
1/4 lb. vermicelli thin spaghetti
   noodles
2 tbs. extra virgin olive oil

zest of 1 lemon
1/2 oz. caviar, any variety,
   domestic or imported

Bring a full pot of water to a boil and salt heavily. Add vermicelli and cook according to directions. Pasta should be firm (al dente), not overcooked. Strain and rinse with cool water. Toss with olive oil and lemon zest. Twist piles of vermicelli into shallow bowls with a coating of lemon broth. Top with a small serving of caviar. Serve pasta warm; broth and caviar should be cool.

LEMON GLASS BROTH WITH SMOKED SALMON TARTARE

Salmon Tartare is named as a cousin to Steak Tartare, where raw beef is seasoned and served with capers, dill or parsley, and onions.

½ lb. whole smoked salmon
½ small red onion, finely chopped
¼ cup fresh dill
1–2 tbs. capers

½ tsp. salt
2 tbs. extra virgin olive oil
Lemon Glass Broth, page 50
chives stems for garnish
cracked pepper

Slice salmon into small cubes (about ¼ x ¼ inch). Toss with onion, dill, capers, salt and olive oil. Spoon mixture into center of lemon broth coated bowl. Serve with thin toasts and a dollop of crème fraiche. Garnish with whole chive stems and season with cracked pepper. Serve cool.

LIGHT LOBSTER BISQUE WITH BASIL

Serves 4–6

A classic rich and heavy soup is lightened up with yogurt instead of cream. Serve with crusty bread and cracked pepper.

1 yellow onion, finely chopped
1 shallot, finely chopped
1 tsp. salt
1 tbs. tomato paste
2 cups fish stock
½ cup dry sherry

½ lb. lobster meat, cooked
   and chopped
1 cup lowfat plain yogurt
¼ cup finely chopped parsley
sprigs fresh basil for garnish
cracked pepper, optional

Sauté onion and shallot with salt over medium heat until soft and translucent. Stir in tomato paste until incorporated. Add fish stock and sherry and bring to a simmer. Add lobster meat to heat through. Remove from heat and stir in yogurt and parsley. Garnish with basil. Serve warm or cool. Add pepper to season.

WATERCRESS WITH SEARED SCALLOPS

Serves 4–6

The vibrant color and clean flavor of pureed watercress serves as the perfect backdrop for sweet seared scallops.

1 tbs. lemon juice
1 lb. fresh scallops
1 small yellow onion, diced
2 cloves garlic, chopped
extra virgin olive oil

3 cups chicken stock
3 cups fresh watercress
flour to coat
1/4 tsp. hot paprika
salt and pepper to taste

Toss lemon with scallops and marinate for 15 minutes. Sauté onion and garlic in extra virgin olive oil until soft. Add stock and bring to a boil. Add watercress and simmer until soft and fragrant. Cool slightly. Puree until smooth. Pat scallops dry. Coat with flour and paprika. Sear in a hot skillet until deep brown (about 2 minutes each side). Place 3 scallops at the bottom of each bowl. Pour watercress broth around scallops. Do not submerge. Serve warm.

YELLOW CURRY WITH MUSSELS AND RICE   Serves 4–6

Derived from paella, this is a light and easy lunch or dinner. Rice soaks up the vibrant yellow of the spicy curry, which complements sweet mussels perfectly.

2 tbs. yellow curry powder
2 cups coconut milk
1 small red bell pepper, seeded and diced
1/2 cucumber, peeled, seeded and diced

1/2 cup short grain rice, uncooked
2 cups chicken broth
1 lb. fresh mussels, debearded and cleaned
1/2 cup fresh basil, cut into strips

Simmer all ingredients but mussels over low heat for 20 to 30 minutes, or until rice is cooked. Add mussels and cover until mussel shells open. Discard any mussels that don't open. Garnish with basil. Serve warm.

SPICY COCONUT BROTH WITH SEARED SHRIMP AND BASIL

Serves 4–6

This intensely flavorful broth appreciates the mildly sweet shrimp and basil. Serve with summer rolls or Thai noodles.

2 cups coconut milk
2 cups fish or chicken broth
1 tsp. grated fresh ginger
2 cloves garlic, minced
1 small jalapeño or other spicy pepper, seeded and minced

1 tbs. yellow madras curry powder
Seared Shrimp, page 19
1/4 cup fresh basil, cut into long strips (chiffonade)

Combine coconut milk, broth, ginger, garlic, jalapeño and curry powder. Simmer over medium heat for 20 minutes. Add salt and pepper to taste.

Add shrimp and garnish with basil. Serve warm.

SUMMER FISHERMAN'S CHOWDER

Serves 4–6

Use any combination of the suggested fish for this summer meal.

1 small yellow onion, diced
3 cloves garlic, minced
extra virgin olive oil
3 cups fish stock or clam juice
1/2 cup white wine
1 tsp. Old Bay seasoning
1 tbs. tomato paste
1 Yukon Gold potato, diced

2 large tomatoes, chopped
1/2 lb. shellfish (scallops, clams, mussels)
1/2 lb. meaty white fish (shrimp, tuna or other), diced
salt and pepper to taste
1/2 cup basil, cut into long strips (chiffonade)

Sauté onion and garlic in oil until soft. Add stock, wine, seasoning and tomato paste; bring to a simmer. Add potato and simmer until soft. Add tomatoes and seafood and simmer until shellfish opens, shrimp are pink and fish is opaque and firm. Discard unopened shellfish. Serve warm, with crusty bread.

SUMMER CORN CHOWDER

Fresh summer corn makes the difference in this light and flavorful chowder. Try serving with a Caprese salad of fresh mozzarella, basil and tomatoes with olive oil and balsamic vinegar.

1 leek, white only, chopped
2 cloves garlic, chopped
extra virgin olive oil
8 ears of corn, shucked and
    cleaned

2 cups chicken stock
1/2 cup nonfat or lowfat yogurt
1/2 cup lump crab meat
1/2 cup fresh basil, cut into strips
salt and pepper to taste

Sauté leek and garlic in extra virgin olive oil until soft. Slice corn from cobs over a wide bowl. Add chicken stock to leeks and bring to a simmer. Add half of the corn kernels and simmer for 3 minutes. Puree mixture until smooth. Return to pan, add remaining corn, yogurt and crab meat. Simmer and season to taste. Garnish with basil and season with salt and pepper. Serve warm.

LEMON BROTH WITH ARTICHOKES

Serves 4–6

This clear broth, like other clear broths and teas, can be served unclouded as a base for garnishes. Clear broths are generally prepared and seasoned separately from other ingredients and assembled right before serving. They should never be left to sit for long periods of time with starchy ingredients such as pasta or potatoes as they will cloud up and lose their appeal.

1 cup artichoke hearts, fresh or canned, chopped
Lemon Glass Broth, page 50
cracked pepper
1/2 cup parsley, chopped

Add artichoke hearts to *Lemon Glass Broth* and simmer gently. Season to taste with pepper and garnish with parsley. Serve warm or cool.

GINGER MISO WITH ASIAN NOODLES AND WAKAME

Serves 4–6

Wakame is a kind of seaweed. It is very commonly used in Japanese salads.

4 tbs. miso paste (or follow instructions on package to make
    4 cups miso soup)
4 cups water
1 tsp. grated fresh ginger
1/4 cup dried wakame
1/2 lb. udon, rice or soba noodles

Dissolve miso in hot water. Add ginger and wakame and simmer until wakame is soft. Boil Asian noodles of choice according to directions. Toss cooked noodles with sesame oil and add to broth right before serving. Serve warm.

BEET BROTH WITH BLOOD ORANGE SALSA   Serves 4–6

Clean and bright, this summer soup captures the best of a classic borscht paired with an unusual salad. Without being weighted down by cream, the fresh flavors of summer produce shine here.

1 lb. fresh red beets, peeled	4–6 blood or regular oranges,
3 cups water	segmented, pith removed
1 tsp. grated fresh ginger	1 tbs. extra virgin olive oil
juice of 1/2 lemon	1/2 cup finely chopped parsley
2 tbs. honey	salt and pepper to taste
1/2 tsp. salt	

Slice beets and cover with water in a pan. Add ginger, lemon, honey and salt. Simmer, uncovered, until beets are soft.

Combine orange segments, olive oil, parsley and a dash of salt and pepper. Serve beet broth in wide bowls; add orange salsa right before serving. Serve cool.

GREEN TEA BROTH
WITH PEAS, MINT AND RICE

Serves 4–6

If you are in a hurry, try using steamed rice from your local Chinese take-out. The flavor and texture are great for this dish.

4 cups water
½ tsp. grated fresh ginger
4 green tea bags
1 cup steamed rice
1 tbs. extra virgin olive oil

½ tsp. salt
1 cup fresh or frozen peas
¼ cup fresh mint, chopped
cracked pepper

Bring water and ginger to a simmer. Add tea bags, steep for 5 minutes and remove tea bags.

Cook rice separately: add oil and salt to rice water. Add peas when rice is just about done and cook through. Toss cooked rice with fresh mint and cracked pepper. Add rice and pea mixture to center of soup bowls right before serving. Serve cool or warm.

TILAPIA POACHED IN BLACK TEA BROTH WITH GREENS AND MUSHROOMS

Serves 4–6

The earthy tea and mushrooms balance the bitter greens and slightly sweet fish. The result is spa food at its finest.

1 cup sliced shitake mushrooms
2 cloves garlic, chopped
extra virgin olive oil
2 cups water
2 cups chicken broth
4 black tea bags
½ lb. fresh tilapia, sliced (or use flounder or sole)
1 packed cup arugala or escarole leaves
salt and pepper to taste

Sauté mushrooms and garlic in extra virgin olive oil until soft and fragrant. Add water and chicken broth and bring to a simmer. Add tea bags and steep for 5 minutes. Remove tea bags, add fish and greens and simmer until fish is opaque and greens are wilted. Season with salt and pepper and serve warm or cool.

JASMINE TEA BROTH
WITH FIGS AND HONEY

Serves 4–6

This is what you might call a dessert soup. Jasmine brings out the floral quality of fresh figs. Both are naturally complimented by honey. This is a simple and elegant combination. Like many broths, this broth freezes well. Try filling ice cube trays with leftovers then storing the cubes in freezer storage bags for up to 3 months.

4 cups water
4 jasmine tea bags
2 cups fresh figs, quartered
2 tbs. honey

Bring water to a simmer and turn off heat. Add tea bags and figs. Let sit for 5 minutes and remove tea bags. Spoon into bowls and drizzle with honey before serving. Serve cool or warm.

CHILI-LIME BROTH WITH FLANK STEAK

Serves 4–6

This very simple soup with Mexican roots is perfect with tortilla chips and a fresh green salad dressed with lime and olive oil.

1 lb. flank steak	1 small yellow onion, chopped
2 tbs. chili powder	3 cloves garlic, minced
juice and zest of 2 limes	3 cups beef broth
extra virgin olive oil	salt and pepper to taste

Rub steak with half of the chili powder and half of the lime juice. Grill over high heat until seared and cooked to your liking. Let rest. Sauté onion and garlic in oil until soft. Add remaining chili powder and stir until a paste forms. Add more olive oil if necessary. Add ¼ cup broth and stir until chili paste is dissolved. Add remaining broth and simmer for 10 minutes. Add remaining lime juice and zest to broth. Slice steak thinly against the grain. Serve warm with broth. Season with salt and pepper.

GRILLED CHICKEN WITH FENNEL BROTH

Serves 4–6

This soup is light and healthy, packed with lean protein and potassium. Stir before serving to eliminate any solidified olive oil.

2–3 chicken breast fillets
extra virgin olive oil
salt and pepper to taste
1 small yellow onion, diced
2 cloves garlic, minced
3 cups chicken broth
1 bunch watercress
1/2 tsp. salt
1/2 small bulb fresh fennel, thinly sliced
1/2 lemon
1/4 cup fresh parsley, finely chopped

Coat chicken with extra virgin olive oil, salt and pepper. Grill until cooked through. (Pan searing is a good alternative if a grill is not available.) Let rest.

Sauté onion and garlic in olive oil until soft. Add chicken broth and bring to a simmer. Add watercress and $1/2$ tsp. salt and cook for 2 to 3 minutes. Puree mixture until smooth.

Return to pan and simmer. Add more broth if necessary. Add fennel and simmer until soft. Slice chicken against the grain and place into bowls of broth. Season with fresh cracked pepper, a squeeze of lemon and a drizzle of extra virgin olive oil. Garnish with parsley. Serve with crusty bread. Serve warm.

SPICED BEEF SOUP
WITH LIME-RICE NOODLES

Serves 4–6

Based on the Vietnamese soup Pho, this is light and flavorful. If desired, add slices of raw beef to bowls before ladling hot broth.

1 small yellow onion, chopped
2 cloves garlic, minced
4 cups beef stock
1 tsp. grated fresh ginger
1 star anise
3 whole cloves
1 cinnamon stick

1 cardamom pod, optional
6 oz. rice noodles
1 scallion, chopped
juice and zest of 1 lime
1/4 cup fresh basil, cut into strips
1/2 cup bean sprouts for garnish

Sauté onion and garlic in oil until soft. Add broth and spices and simmer for 30 minutes. Strain broth. Add noodles and scallion. Simmer until noodles are cooked through. Add lime juice and zest. Serve warm and garnish with basil and bean sprouts.

INDEX